Service
Excellence!

Here's the straight truth about customer service –
the good, the bad and the ugly. No propaganda.
No goody-two-shoes thinking. Just an honest look
at what it's like out there in the real world where
you work every day.

Call them what you want – customers...passen-
gers...patients...clients...These are the people who
buy and use the products you sell or the services
you provide. Sometimes they make work a pleasure, and sometimes they're hard as nails. Day in,
day out, they make you earn your money.

Well, here's how to make a hard job a whole lot
easier.

This isn't a boring book of rules. You won't
run into complicated concepts, and you won't find
a preachy list of "shoulds" and "ought to's." What
you get is 31 pages packed with raw truth.

This is stuff you can use.

You want to be good—really good—at what
you do? Just read this booklet, and put these ideas
to work.

PRITCHETT & ASSOCIATES, INC.

Table of Contents

Maybe you didn't really plan on it...maybe you did. But you have ended up in one of the toughest jobs around.

Dealing with clients and customers is not like working with "things." It's very different from solitary work where you're putting parts together, playing with ideas, running a piece of equipment, or wrestling with numbers off by yourself.

In customer service you're working with moods, tempers, expectations, and misunderstandings. You're dealing with personalities...human beings. You have to cope with their headaches, hormones, and personal hangups. It can be a brutal job.

People who work alone don't have these hassles.

Physical Labor Versus Emotional Labor

Some jobs are tough because of the physical labor involved. People have to lift or load things, move stuff, be up and down, stay on their feet, or constantly be on the go. There is probably some of this involved in your job, too. But that's not why your job is so hard.

> Customer service is heavy-duty work because of the *psychological* energy it consumes.

The social effort you have to put forth hour after hour, day after day, represents a tremendous amount of emotional labor.

You have to meet and greet people, control your attitude, plus make an effort to understand, serve, and satisfy. There's a lot of mental and psychological work involved in that. Of

1

course, working with people can be enjoyable, even refreshing, when it goes well. But you still have to invest energy in the process.

The emotional cost is much greater when clients and customers are unappreciative, unrealistic, and uncooperative. Sometimes they are nasty-tempered and demanding, maybe even dishonest and demeaning. Some like to have fun at your expense. Some seem dumb and misinformed.

Dealing with this doesn't require much *physical energy,* but it's a real drain on your *psychological energy.* Eventually it can lead to emotional fatigue.

Burnout

Customer service makes heavy demands of the spirit. Facing the same sort of people and problems, month after month, can deaden your heart and dull your senses. The customers begin to look the same and sound alike. Yet each person feels he or she is special, different, and deserving of your best efforts.

If you reach the point of being used up and burned out from too much emotional labor, your work will show it. You get a little tired of trying. You move through the workday on automatic pilot. You go through the motions, and the job gets done, but your heart really isn't in it. Service quality begins to slip. Then customers react negatively to that, and your job gets even harder.

It can become a vicious cycle where everybody loses— you, the organization, and the customer all become victims. But it doesn't have to go that way.

Life On The Front Lines

You're out there fighting where the wars to win and keep customers are either won or lost. It's tough duty being a foot soldier for service excellence.

It's also a make-or-break situation for the organization. Customers measure the quality of the firm by the quality of your service. In their eyes, you *are* the organization. You shape its reputation, bit by bit, all day long.

Without paying customers, nobody has a job. The organization will shrink, wither and eventually die unless there are people willing to pay for what you do. Customers vote daily on how well you do your job, and they vote with their money. If your competitors serve the paying customers better, you lose the vote.

Nobody else in the organization is in a position to do your job. Other people aren't in the right place at the right time. They can't make it happen.

The organization has to depend on you.

Sometimes you probably feel like a victim of circumstances.

Your organization's quality of service depends on a variety of factors, and many of these lie beyond your control. Situations can develop, through no fault of your own, where you have to fight an uphill battle to please customers. You have to cope with the results, but you're not in a position to get rid of the causes.

Working Around The Roadblocks

Let's examine seven potential roadblocks you may have to maneuver around in search of service excellence.

Obstacle Number One: Product Quality Problems

Your job gets tough when the goods aren't very good.

Usually customer satisfaction is directly affected by the quality of the product itself. It might be a bad hamburger, unreliable automobile, or airplane delayed by mechanical problems. Regardless of whether the problem was created by someone else, or just caused by circumstances, you end up having to handle the customer complaints.

Product quality problems can leave you with a salvage operation on your hands. The situation calls for a last ditch effort, because the organization's reputation is riding on you.

At that particular point in time, outstanding service is the only hope for getting around the product quality roadblock.

Obstacle Number Two: Fouled-Up Systems and Procedures

Customer service takes a beating when the way things work doesn't work well at all.

Organizations sometimes cripple along, making service excellence a real struggle because the necessary work guidelines aren't in place, policies are inefficient, or rules are too rigid. Standard operating procedures are not always designed to be "customer friendly."

You're right there on the firing line, and you're going to have to make some judgment calls. If rules and procedures are getting in the way of customer service, maybe it's time to bend them a little. And maybe you should push to get them changed.

> You've got to have the guts to stand up
> for the customer instead of defending rules
> that get in the way.

You have to use your head and think for yourself.

Obstacle Number Three: Inadequate Equipment and Supplies

It may feel like you are being asked to build castles without tools.

Customer service gets complicated when the organization doesn't provide the necessary equipment and supplies. Your effectiveness is restricted if you don't have the gear you need.

It may be inadequate inventory of spare parts, an outdated phone system, not enough computers, too few checkout lines, or some other deficiency. From your position, it may look like the organization is being "penny wise and pound foolish" in not spending the money to equip you properly for service excellence.

Maybe it helps to remember that some of the world's most magnificent structures were built without sophisticated equip-

6

ment and elaborate materials. It was the efforts of *people* that made possible the pyramids, the great cathedrals, and other monuments of the ancient world.

Your job has glory potential, too.

> ## It's possible for one person, acting alone, to deliver monumental customer service.

You can be a star. Usually the legends of service excellence are the stories of how one individual took on the challenge of a critical customer problem and, singlehandedly, overcame the odds.

Obstacle Number Four: Work Overload

Sometimes clients and customers all seem to hit at once. Lines form. Lights blink as calls start backing up. Pressure mounts as people get restless and impatient.

There's more to do than you can handle. You're outnumbered. You think, "Never has so much been done for so many by so few."

Being overworked and understaffed can really put you in a corner as you try to serve clients and customers.

You can't give people the time they need. You're spread too thin. This situation usually results in buck-passing, unresponsiveness, and superficial problem-solving.

The challenge is to maintain a good attitude, to show grace under pressure. Keep in mind that if it's a bad situation for you, it's probably a worse situation for the customer.

Obstacle Number Five: Lack of Job Know-How

Trying to serve clients and customers when you haven't been properly trained is like the blind leading the blind.

You can't fake service excellence for long. And it's not enough to be well-intentioned in your efforts—you need to be able to answer questions and solve problems.

Job knowledge is a key requirement for service excellence. If the organization fails to provide the necessary training and coaching, you may not possess the know-how to handle customer needs effectively.

This booklet gives you a solid set of ground rules for handling the people aspects of customer service. Study these ideas, follow them to the letter, and you will be close to service excellence.

You can also show initiative and assume personal responsibility for learning the technical side of your job. Your efforts will benefit you even more than the organization.

Obstacle Number Six: Coworkers that Cop Out

Service excellence becomes a burden when you have to carry somebody else's load. Make sure nobody is having to carry part of yours.

Of course, an organization's reputation for customer service, good or bad, is built by everybody who works in the place. It's also true that front-line customer contact employees can't do it all. Your coworkers' efforts have a direct impact on your chances for success in serving clients.

That can be a problem, because it's easy for some departments and work groups deep inside the firm to lose sight of the customer. When they fail to offer the support they should toward service excellence, you can get caught in the middle. You may end up carrying somebody else's load.

Karl Albrecht, author of *Service America!,* writes,

"If you're not serving the customer, you'd better be serving someone who is."

Help get this idea across to your coworkers in other parts of the organization.

8

Obstacle Number Seven: A Corporate Culture That Doesn't Care

You run into another roadblock to service excellence when you have to cope with a cult of mediocrity.

The standards of performance an organization sets for itself sometimes leave a lot to be desired. Some firms routinely produce shoddy products and accept shabby treatment of customers.

If the corporate culture reflects low standards—a widespread shortage of organizational pride—it's difficult for you to deliver high quality service on a consistent basis.

You have to become a missionary, a zealot, a fanatic, if you want to influence the service attitudes of others in the organization.

You have to be passionate in pursuit of service excellence if you want to overcome a corporate cult of mediocrity.

Damage Control

It can be very aggravating when other people or external circumstances cause unnecessary problems and complicate your job. It's a pain having to clean up somebody else's mess.

But service excellence always involves some degree of damage control. That just goes with the territory. That's just the way it is in the real world.

Why should you try? Why struggle to take up the slack left by somebody else? Why fight to get around the roadblocks?

The hard reality is this: that's your job. Nobody else is in a position to do what you can. You're close to the action. When the organization slips up somehow, you can do the most to help it recover.

You're the ace in the hole.

Let's look at the situation from your point of view.

Going all out in search of service excellence sounds like a lot more work. So the idea isn't very appealing if you're already really trying.

The Selling Point

It's not easy to get pumped up about helping the organization build a top-notch reputation for customer service if it means more struggle and strain on your part. You may feel like clients or customers don't appreciate your present efforts like they should. It may seem higher management just takes you for granted. So what's the argument for putting forth more effort?

Well, here's the point:

> Service *excellence* doesn't require
> as much emotional labor as service *mediocrity*.

We're talking about what happens when you start working smarter, not harder. Service excellence is a smart concept. It creates the kind of situation where everybody wins.

Your payoff is that the job gets easier.

The Path of Least Resistance

Don't make your job harder than it has to be.

A common mistake is to interact with customers in ways

that actually increase the emotional labor. But striving for service excellence helps prevent, or at least minimizes, the interpersonal hassles of your job. It helps you avoid attitude burnout. Instead of wanting to psychologically unplug from your job, you can take pleasure in what you're doing.

Sincere efforts to deliver excellent service are easy to spot. Customers know this kind of behavior when they see it. The truth is they don't get a chance to experience it very often. So when you give them special treatment, it really grabs their attention.

Service excellence puts you and the customer on the same side. Instead of being adversaries, you become partners. If your behavior makes it clear that your intent is to do battle *for* them and not *against* them, you have the basis for successful and satisfying relationships. You sidestep resistance if you align your efforts with theirs. They may be a little surprised, but they'll like what they see.

So service excellence results in less wear and tear on you. There's not as much psychological energy required in your work because pleasant, cooperative relationships are the easiest to handle.

The approach that gives you the best shot
of taking care of customers is the same one that
best takes care of you.

That's important, since about half of your waking hours are being spent in the work environment. You don't want to spend that much of your day-to-day life with the blahs or being miserable.

If you're committed to providing the best possible customer service, you're following the path of least resistance. There's less job stress because you get better treatment from your customers. Everybody wins.

12

There's another very personal reason for delivering superior customer service:

> ## Doing an excellent job is a lot more satisfying than doing a mediocre job.

At the end of a workday, when all is said and done, you simply feel better when you know you've shown "the right stuff."

Doing quality work is emotionally gratifying. Success feeds the heart. The better you do your job, the better you feel about yourself.

On the other hand, the weaker your personal commitment to the job, the more your spirit starts to sag. The fun fades out of what you do for a living if you give it only a halfhearted effort. That's important to remember, because work that isn't enjoyable requires a lot more emotional labor.

Delivering service excellence, performing so well that you literally surprise customers, will recharge your emotional batteries. It puts a little more bounce in your step, a little more pride in your heart. Your payoff is a psychological energy boost that revs you up and, again, makes the job easier.

Providing outstanding customer service is a way to (1) build your own self-esteem, (2) lift your spirits, and (3) increase your level of job satisfaction. You, personally, can improve your quality of work life.

The first and highest priority in customer service work is to build good relationships with your customers.

Here's why it's so important:

▶ If your customers don't like you, the odds are 100 to 1 they're not going to like your service.

▶ Problems are a lot easier to solve when you're on good terms with the customer.

▶ If the relationship doesn't go well, it not only complicates the basic problem but also creates new headaches.

So the energy it takes to start the relationship off on the right foot is a very wise investment. Just a little extra effort on the front end can prevent some real hassles later on.

Remember, the idea is to reduce the amount of emotional labor in your job. Here's a chance to work smart.

> ## It's much easier to build a good relationship than to struggle with a bad one.

There are three steps involved in managing the relationship. They are so simple, but so powerful. As W. Clement Stone has written, "Success comes from doing common things uncommonly well." Here's how you can build a good relationship.

1. Take the initiative

2. Be positive.

3. Make the customer feel special.

15

That's not very complicated...not much to remember. But there's magic in these three moves. Let's examine each one in more detail.

Take The Initiative.

It is critically important that you make the opening move. In every customer encounter, mobilize yourself and be the first to reach out. The best defense is a good offense.

Seizing the initiative enables you to wield early influence over the other person's behavior. It's like occupying the high ground in battle—you gain the advantage. Use the opportunity to "shape" the customer's attitude and behaviors in the desired direction.

Look at it this way...any time you encounter another person, you get to decide whether you want to *act* or *react.* You have a choice.

Of course, if you fool around too long trying to make up your mind, the other person may take that choice away from you. He or she could decide more quickly and get the jump on you by acting first. In that case, naturally, you're put in a position of having to react. That is *the basic mistake* in customer service work.

You want to be proactive, not reactive.

Obviously you have to be on your toes. But taking the initiative can become a habit.

Be Positive.

Now you have to make another decision. Another choice. Once you have chosen to act, to take the initiative, you must decide *how* you will behave.

You have three options:

1. You can be positive (upbeat, affirming, personable, interested, respectful, and considerate).

16

2. You can be neutral (indifferent, bland, flat, matter-of-fact, or distant).

3. You can be negative (unpleasant, mean, angry, rude, defensive, or uncooperative).

The payoff is in being positive. That's what gets the relationship moving in the right direction.

Here's the key point:

> # When you take the initiative and act positively, you put psychological pressure on the customer to react in a positive fashion.

In a sense, you can obligate the other person to reciprocate with the same type of behavior.

Granted, it doesn't always happen that the other person will respond with similar behavior, but the odds are certainly in your favor. Naturally, you want to receive positive treatment from your customers, so set the stage for it.

It should be emphasized that other people have the privilege of labeling your behavior, because they're on the receiving end. In other words, they will classify your manner as positive, negative or neutral. They will hold you accountable.

For example, if you think you are smiling warmly and they say you have a sarcastic smirk on your face, your behavior will be labeled negative instead of positive. Customers know how it feels to them, and you have to make your behavior work so that they receive a positive feeling.

Sometimes that's not easy because you're feeling out of sorts or have problems of your own. Like a professional athlete, you'll have to "play with pain." Also it's hard to be positive when you're getting rotten treatment from the customer. Being positive may involve some forgiveness on your part, particularly when the customer turns out to be wrong.

17

Here's something to keep in mind:

> When customers are being rude, negative, and generally difficult, the odds are you're not the target, you just happen to be within range.

So don't take it personally when you come under attack. Regardless of how unpleasant a customer is, you can remain positive and professional. It's your choice.

Make The Customer Feel Special.

Now it's time to put a little spin on the ball.

Your first two moves—taking the initiative, and behaving in a positive manner—get you off to a good start in building the right kind of relationship with the customer. But this third move is that "extra touch" you can use to make things roll in the right direction.

Here's an idea you can take to the bank:

> The customers that make you feel special will become special customers.

The idea is to provide such remarkable service that you literally surprise the customer. Make him or her feel "privileged." This means going beyond the call of duty. It's giving more than the customer expects—in the way you relate, and the way you try.

This is easier if you approach each customer as if he or she were your *only* customer, as if this were a person you *must* get to know, satisfy, and keep happy.

Instead of taking customers for granted, over-deliver in the way you serve them. Make them feel important! The people who aren't special will never forget it if you do...and the people who are will never forget it if you don't.

In some customer situations, about the only way you can really shine is in managing the relationship.

Maybe you can't fully take care of the problems or give customers all they ask for. But you can always take the initiative, be positive, and make them feel special. When you do that, it makes customers more tolerant. They become more open-minded and forgiving, plus kinder toward you. They're easier to work with, and that means less emotional labor in your job.

> There's only one way you can effectively manage the behavior of your clients and customers. You do it by managing your own behavior.

Really, all you can control is you. Just yourself. But that's enough, if you do it right.

These guidelines for managing the relationship not only help you win new customers, they let you hang on to the ones you already have.

Manage the Transaction

After setting the stage for a good relationship with the customer, you still have to conduct the business. You have to serve the client's needs or take care of the problem. If you don't manage this business transaction effectively, sooner or later it will damage the relationship.

There are three key steps in managing the transaction:

1. Listen and understand.

2. Be helpful.

3. Deal with the uniqueness of the situation.

Whether customers come to you with routine needs or special problems, you can do your best job of handling the transaction by following these three simple guidelines.

Listen and Understand.

The opening move in managing the transaction amounts to problem identification. So focus in on the customer. Give your undivided attention.

Don't jump to conclusions. Don't prejudge. Don't start placing blame. Don't argue or become defensive. Don't even start solving the problem yet.

Concentrate on getting in tune with the customer, finding the same wavelength. Make that person's point of view your own for the moment. Demonstrate your interest in understanding the situation...*according to the customer's logic!* Establish a common ground by looking at things from his or her perspective. If you were that person, what would you want?

21

Think like a customer!

Sniff out the other person's concerns, wants, and needs. Ask questions. Get the facts. Listen carefully. Try to read between the lines, because customers are frequently confused, lack the necessary facts, or simply are not explaining things well. Determine what's missing—what it will take to satisfy the client.

Also, read what the nonverbal messages say about the customer. Sometimes body language is more important than words.

In this first step toward managing the transaction effectively, you should *go looking for trouble*. That is, welcome bad news. Customer complaints can be a resource, because they point directly toward the possibility of creating a breakthrough experience with the customer. Look for such openings as the really difficult customer, the hairy problem, the big foul-up. These give you a chance to be a hero.

Customer problems always represent a "Window of Opportunity."

Problems give you a chance to leave a mark on the mind of the customer. You can turn them into real opportunities. They represent an opening for you to do something special, to show how you can "recover" for the client and the company.

Be Helpful

Now it's time for you to grab hold and take action. This second step in managing the transaction means you move into gear.

If you've really listened, you now can demonstrate your understanding of the situation. You have a handle on the customer's expectations, wants and needs, or concerns. You can address the top priorities. You know what turns on the customer, what lights that person's fire.

Take *personal* responsibility for satisfying the client. Consider yourself an agent of the customer. For the moment, be on his or her side. Put your heads together and create options. Search for alternatives. Do some joint problem-solving. Keep the focus on resources that can be brought to bear on the situation, because you have a better idea of what's available to work with than the customer does.

The idea at this stage of the game is to fix things. So there's a problem? Take care of it, even if it's a problem the customer caused. No finger-pointing, no runarounds, just an effort that clearly says, "The buck stops here."

You'll always be able to help the client in some way. So even if you can't give what the customer wants, give as much as you can.

Maybe you can bring a new perspective, or offer some encouragement and hope. It's helpful just to let the other person know that you understand the problem and accept it as a difficult situation. It helps to admit mistakes and apologize when your organization is at fault. You're taking action in a helpful fashion just by giving sympathy or showing appreciation.

> If you can't take care of a customer's basic problem, try to take care of the mess it caused.

Give the customer something for the trouble. That is that all-important "second effort" that makes such a strong statement to your customer. You may be able to salvage the relationship, and the customer, simply by making it clear that you really tried.

Deal With the Uniqueness of the Situation

Now for step three in managing the transaction: figure out how this customer is different from all the rest.

What's unique about the person? How is this particular situation special?

When you have spotted the unique aspect of a situation, all of a sudden you have an angle on how to handle it. Now you can customize your approach. Try to be creative. Maybe you can grant special favors, or bend the rules to make things work better. You will know when you need to flex. You can give in when it makes sense to do so.

If it's an unusual request from a customer or client, you have an opening to leave a lasting impression. Don't think of it as an aggravation, but as a valuable window of opportunity. You have a chance to make a hit with the customer. This is one of the important "moments of truth" in customer service.

There never was a customer who liked being just another number. And even though you may have dealt with the very same situation ten times during the last hour, it remains a special and personal matter to each new customer you encounter.

This third step personalizes your efforts to manage the transaction. It's an approach that really sets you apart from the competition in the service experience you create for your customer.

Sometimes you can't give *everything* the customer wants. But every time you can give *some* of the things the customer wants. So contribute what you can.

> If you do enough right things, the customer is very forgiving of the things you do wrong.

In your efforts to manage the transaction successfully, never dodge problems. Use them!

People who have had their problems and complaints handled effectively will become your most loyal customers...and probably your most pleasant ones. They will trust you and believe in you. They will depend on you. You will have proven yourself under fire.

Frankly, customers don't expect you or the organization to always do things perfectly. They can accept some mistakes, and they understand that things occasionally go wrong. How you recover is what counts.

So when you fall the hardest, you can bounce the highest.

It's common for an organization to draw up a long, involved list of rules about how to deal with customers. The employees become preoccupied with following the rules and fail to concentrate on what's really important.

You can't just go through a drill you've been taught and assume that means you've met your responsibility to the customer.

Frankly, customers don't give a hoot about the drill. Often they're not particularly impressed when employees follow a list of rules, because they can tell—

...the smile is a fake,

...the employee is mouthing the right words, but isn't interested at all,

...the questions are "canned" and impersonal,

...the "Thank you, please come back" is not authentic.

The truth is...

> Excellent customer service rarely comes from following a rigid list of rules about what to do or say.

Don't get so mentally locked in on the drill that you end up serving the rule system instead of serving your customers. Remember what really counts to clients and customers:

1. Personalized attention—being treated like an individual with very personal needs and a unique situation

2. Positive behavior—respect, consideration, concern, appreciation...in general, some "TLC"

3. Being understood—their feelings, their point of view, and the facts of the situation

4. Helpfulness—results!

Precisely how you go about delivering this isn't all that important to customers.

> ## Service excellence means giving what really counts to the customer.

Always Follow The Game Plan

It's still important, though, to follow an overall strategy. So let's review the strategies for service excellence, and the three steps involved in each one.

Strategy Number One: **Manage The Relationship**

▶ Take the initiative

▶ Be positive.

▶ Make the customer feel special.

Strategy Number Two: **Manage The Transaction**

▶ Listen and understand.

▶ Be helpful.

▶ Deal with the uniqueness of the situation.

These strategic guidelines are the proven techniques that serve as your broad game plan. The details of how that game plan gets carried out are your responsibility. You are the person who must call the various plays as you interact one-on-one with your customers.

There are many different approaches you could use to seize the initiative, be positive, and make customers feel special. Likewise, various alternatives would work as you try to understand, offer help, and show respect for what's unique about the situation.

So how does a person decide what to actually do to implement these strategic guidelines?

Play To Your Strengths

If you want to be a pro in the way you deliver customer service, you must call the plays that you, personally, run the best. Find the behavior that plays to your personal strengths, and you have found your own "magic touch."

The idea is to give the customer the best service performance you can. In order to do that, you have to rely on your best talents. They offer the most promise for a high-powered performance in the way you handle clients and customers.

Do What Comes Naturally

The interpersonal tactics that work best for you will be somewhat unique, a little (or maybe a lot) different from what works best for your coworkers.

Let's face it. Different things work for different people.

Maybe you're not a smiler, or enthusiastic, or particularly good at remembering names. Maybe your strong suit is in being sincere, or making eye contact, or really paying attention.

If you're basically an introvert, nobody's likely to succeed at turning you into a bubbly, outgoing extrovert in the way you serve clients and customers. If you have a serious, subdued temperament, why go through the struggle of trying to act like you have a sparkling disposition? You will have a tough time pulling it off successfully and, besides, it just isn't necessary. In fact, it's a misguided effort. It's throwing your psychological energy in the wrong direction, creating more emotional labor for yourself.

Think about what works for you—what more or less comes naturally, what you do well, and what doesn't require any unusual extra effort. Why not play the ball from the easiest angle?

> The key to service excellence,
> as you deliver it, is to know your personal
> strengths and play them to the hilt.

Don't try to be somebody else. Service excellence, as you provide it, will reflect your individual style...your very own "magic touch."

30

Well, that's it.

Now get out there and give these ideas a test run. But don't feel like you've got to get it perfect the first time around. It takes a while to get your moves down.

No problem—you've got plenty of customers to practice on. Just keep at it. You'll get better and better. *Fast!* And the better you get, the easier your job gets. Plus, you'll get a lot more enjoyment out of what you do!

Wait a couple of days and read this again, front to back. Then thumb through it frequently, until you have the ideas down so well they just become a natural part of the way you go about your job.

You're going to get hooked on service excellence!

31

About the Author

Price Pritchett is Chairman and CEO of Pritchett & Associates, Inc., a Dallas-based firm specializing in organizational change. He has authored more than 20 books on individual and organizational performance, and is recognized internationally as a leading authority on the dynamics of change. He holds a Ph.D. in psychology and has consulted to major corporations for over two decades. Dr. Pritchett's firm has proven expertise in helping organizations upgrade customer service and build sales, even during the difficulties of major change.

ORDER FORM

Service Excellence!

1-99 copies	____ copies at $5.95 each
100-999 copies	____ copies at $5.75 each
1,000-4,999 copies	____ copies at $5.50 each
5,000-9,999 copies	____ copies at $5.25 each
10,000 or more copies	____ copies at $5.00 each

Name _____

Job Title _____

Organization _____

Street Address _____

P.O. Box _____

City, State _____ Zip _____

Country _____

Phone _____

Purchase order number (if applicable) _____

Applicable sales tax, shipping and handling charges will be added. Prices subject to change.

Orders less than $100 require prepayment. $100 or more may be invoiced.

☐ Check Enclosed   ☐ Please Invoice

☐ VISA   ☐ MasterCard   ☐ AMERICAN EXPRESS

Account Number _____ Expiration Date _____

Signature _____

To order, call: 800-992-5922
fax: 972-789-7900
e-mail: http://www.PritchettNet.com/order
or mail this form to the address below

PRITCHETT & ASSOCIATES, INC.

13155 Noel Road, Suite 1600, Dallas, Texas 75240
http://www.PritchettNet.com

EE7298

Management Consulting Services

Pritchett & Associates' global management consultants help clients successfully plan and implement large-scale strategic change. We've been improving the competitiveness of both large and small companies for over two decades—combining our knowledge and experience with an analytic, results-oriented project management approach.

Our consulting group will help you:
- Capitalize on new synergies during difficult merger and joint venture integrations
- Outsource processes/functions to re-focus on core competencies
- Face the organizational challenges associated with the implementation of new information technology
- Redirect your culture to foresee and maximize strategic possibilities
- Create the architecture for continued success and competitive advantage

> **If you would like to talk to one of our consultants about your unique change-related challenges, please call us at 1-888-852-1250.**

Training Programs to Implement Change

Pritchett & Associates' training programs build on the hard-hitting principles in our best-selling handbooks. These quick-impact, concentrated programs have been successfully used by organizations worldwide. They deliver a no-nonsense message on how to deal with today's rapidly changing business environment.

Our training programs will help your organization:
- Recognize the predictable dynamics of change
- Convert "change resisters" to "change agents"
- Improve operating effectiveness and productivity
- Shorten the high-risk transition period
- Keep people focused on the "high priority" issues
- Restore stability and morale

> ***Service Excellence* training program can be customized for your organization. For more information, call 1-800-992-5922.**